HABARI GANI?

(How are you?)

MAMA, BABA AND MPENDWA!

(Loved ones)

Positive Messages for Black Children is a *message storybook* intended to shape our children's thinking about our culture, families, community, people, race, and health. Positive Messages for Black Children complements our activity book **Positive Messages to Uplift and Empower Black Children**. The messages originally produced in the activity book were designed to support mamas, babas, and mpendwa with positive messages to contemplate, recite and discuss with our children.

The messages are so important we want to make them available as a *message storybook* for our children to hear and see the images over and over again. We want our children to continuously visualize and think about their role in uplifting our people collectively. We also want them to be able to enjoy these positive messages on a daily basis through our rich oral tradition of storytelling.

Our children must hear positive messages regularly that will instill a sense of pride, duty and responsibility to themselves, their families, their communities, their people and their race. Our children must know they come from a great ancestral homeland, ancestors who are brilliant and accomplished, and has worked for them to have a better life. Our children must know they have to use their knowledge, talents, skills and resources for our collective upliftment.

Positive Messages for Black Children reinforces messages that let our children know that they come from greatness, that they are great and that they must do great things for themselves, their families, their community, their people, and their race!

WE HOPE THE MESSAGES EMPOWER YOU!

My ancestors are from Africa and made important contributions to the world and so can I.

Black boys are
brilliant, handsome
and talented.

I love my culture because it guides me and provides me with direction.

I love to see my brothers
and sisters play African
drums and dance.

KWANZAA
THE PHILOSOPHY AND OPINIONS OF MARCUS GARVEY
WAKE UP & RISE UP SISTAHS
TELLING TIME
THE MIS-EDUCATION OF THE NEGRO
AFROCENTRICITY
BLACKS IN SCIENCE: ANCIENT AND MODERN
MY DADDY LOVES ME
URBAN PHILOSOPHY
COUNTING IN KIWAHILI
I am going to use
my education to
uplift my family,
community and race.

I love my family and
I am going to make
them proud of me.

Black girls are smart, beautiful and talented.

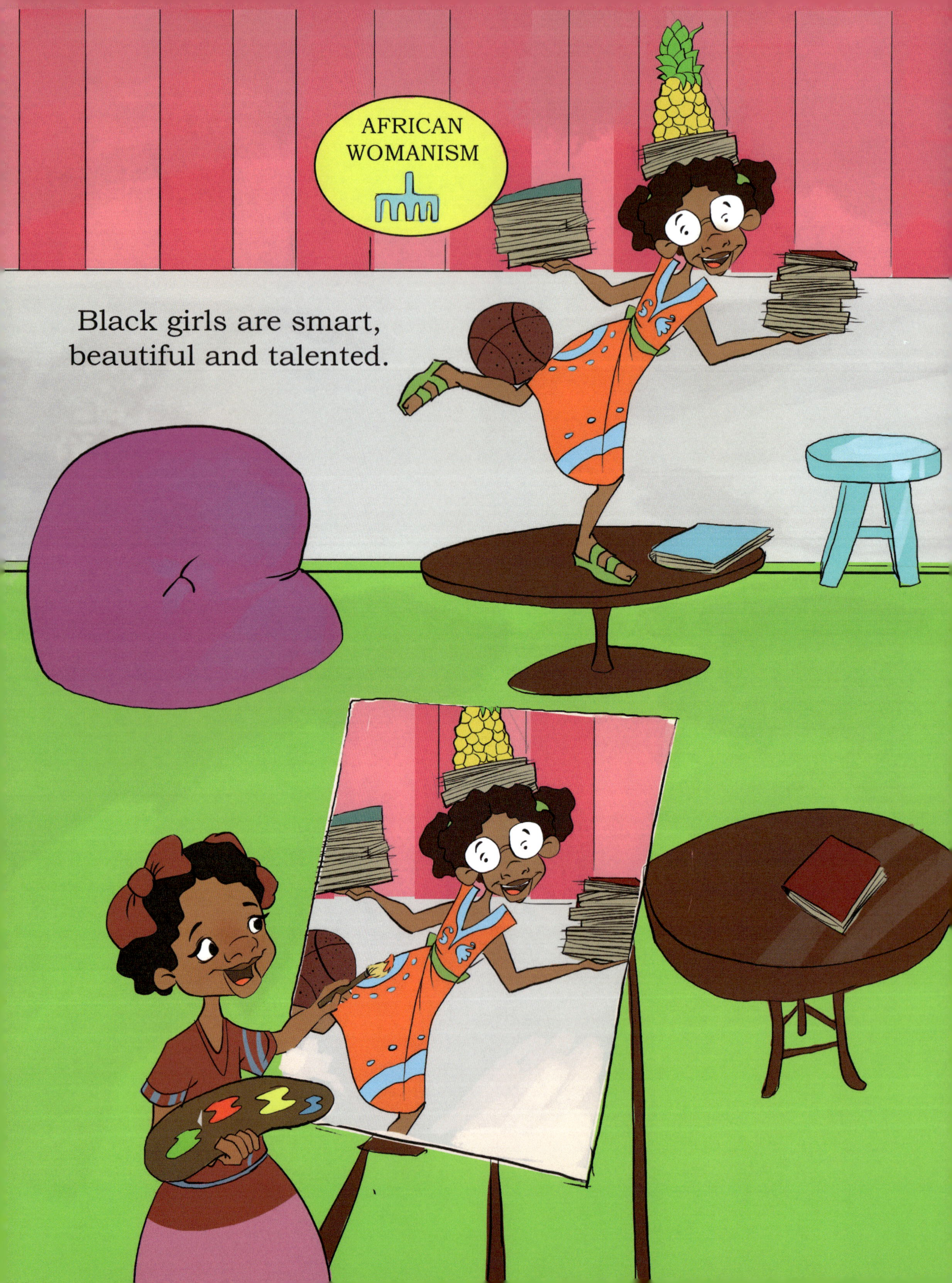

I love to help my
family clean our home.

I am inspired by the contributions and accomplishments of Black people.
GEORGE WASHINGTON CARVER
BENJAMIN BANNEKER
PAUL WILLIAMS
SARAH BOONE
LEWIS LATIMER

I like jogging at school because it helps me stay healthy.

I love learning about my ancestors who were kings in Africa.

I love my family, community and race.

Telling Time Sundial
5 − 3² =
1+1
I love learning and doing math.

If you believe in your nia (purpose), there is no end to what you can achieve.

I am going to work with a Black organization that is committed to improving the conditions of our people.

I love to read, write and listen to poetry.

I love learning about my ancestors who were queens in Africa.
CANDACE QUEEN OF ETHIOPIA
MAKEDA QUEEN OF SHEBA
AMINA
QUEEN OF ZARIA

I love reading books about
Black history and culture.

I love learning about science and conducting experiments.

I am going to travel to Africa to learn more about my ancestral homeland.

We are working to achieve umoja (unity) in our family, community and race.
AFRICAN SOVEREIGNTY COMMUNITY GARDEN

I am being raised in a village of mamas and babas who love me.

I love to drink water because it is good for my body.

In Africa, our ancestors created different types of xylophones to play uplifting music for our people.

I love to eat yams from Africa because they are good for me.

I am in training to be a warrior
for my people in the spirit of my
African ancestor Shaka Zulu.

ABOUT THE AUTHORS

Family Afrika is a Black family that lives in Baltimore, Maryland. They believe in the importance of Black families and children connecting, honoring and respecting our cultural heritage and traditions in Africa, America, the Caribbean, and the Diaspora. As a family, we work hard to learn about our cultural heritage and traditions. We practice the Nguzo Saba (The 7 Principles of Blackness) in our everyday lives and give back to our community.

The stories presented in our books are fictionalized accounts based on real events in our family and our journey to live a life that connects, honors, and respects our cultural heritage and traditions. Reading should be a regular occurrence in Black families, and it is important for Black children to see images that look like them in the books they read.

Becoming parents and watching our son, Sekou, grow up inspired these books and the stories in them. Sekou is co-author because he has contributed greatly to the books. Mama and Baba use his name as co-authors of the books to honor his contributions. We use Afrika as our last name to represent our quest to positively uplift our cultural heritage and traditions originating in Africa. Sekou has inspired us to live a life that more closely reflects our beliefs and political ideology. We strongly believe we have to create Black institutions to positively uplift Black families and children, and connect them to their cultural heritage and traditions.

Baba Sekou Afrika, Ed.D. (also known as Julius Davis) is an associate professor of mathematics education at Bowie State University. His scholarship and advocacy focuses on the intellectual and social development of Black boys and young men. He has studied and traveled to Malawi, Tanzania, and Ethiopia on the continent of Africa to learn more about our cultural heritage and traditions.

Mama Sekou Afrika (also known as Yolanda Davis) is a clinical research professional who has studied and traveled to Senegal on the continent of Africa and the Caribbean Islands to learn more about our cultural heritage and traditions.

Sekou Afrika (also known as Sekou Davis) is a student at Ujamaa Shule, the oldest independent Afrikan School in the United States. He plays the Afrikan drums with his brothers and sisters at Ujamaa. To start his formal school-based academic and social development, Sekou attended Watoto Development Center in Baltimore, MD, an Afrikan-centered institution.

Asante Sana (Thank you very much) for practicing Ujamaa (cooperative economics) by purchasing this book and supporting our Black-owned family business. A portion of the proceeds from this book will be used to support and sponsor efforts to culturally uplift Black children and families.

Your Support is Greatly Appreciated!

Baba Sekou Afrika, Mama Sekou Afrika, Sekou Afrika

KUJICHAGULIA PRESS

We define, speak and create for ourselves to celebrate our African and African American cultural heritage and uplift our people using our Kuumba (creativity).

Title: Positive Messages for Black Children
Written by: Baba Sekou Afrika, Mama Sekou Afrika, and Sekou Afrika
Edited By: Nadirah Angail
Illustration & Design by: Eloy Claudio

Summary: This message storybook is intended to shape our children's thinking about our culture, families, community, people, race and health.

ISBN: 978-0-9964595-5-6
For more information or to book an event,
contact Baba/Mama Sekou at books@kujichaguliapress.com.

Kujichagulia Press
P.O. Box 31766
Baltimore, MD 21207
www.kujichaguliapress.com

KujichaguliaPress

KujichaguliaPress

@Kujichaguliaprs

#PositiveMessages
#Uplift
#Empower
#BlackChildren

Made in the USA
Columbia, SC
20 November 2017